Circumnavigation

Acknowledgements
Thanks are due to the editors of the following publications
in which some of these poems have appeared: *Brando's Hat,
The North, Pitch, The Rialto, Smiths Knoll, Staple, Tears in
the Fence, Fenland* (Blue Nose Poets 2001), *Poems 23* (Lancaster Literature Festival 2000)

Circumnavigation was the overall winner in The Poetry
Business Book & Pamphlet Competition 2001

Circumnavigation

Jane Routh

Smith/Doorstop Books

i.m. Dorothy

Published 2002 by
Smith/Doorstop Books
The Poetry Business
The Studio
Byram Arcade
Westgate
Huddersfield HD1 1ND

ISBN 1-902382-43-9

British Library Cataloguing-in-Publication Data. A catalogue
record for this book is available from the British Library.

Typeset at The Poetry Business
Printed by Peepal Tree Press, Leeds
Cover photo by Jane Routh
Author's photo by Mike Barlow

Distributed by Central Books, 99 Wallis Road, London E9 5LN

The Poetry Business gratefully acknowledges the help of
Kirklees Metropolitan Council and Yorkshire Arts.

CONTENTS

Still Life with Loch Fyne Skiff

For a headland, the dark slope of the valley;
for a lighthouse, the yard light over at Birks,
occluding, random
whenever a gust bows the cherry tree down.
Tissue paper on the windowsill
crumples like breakers:
a shoreline.

Her sails are a black triangle
lost on a night's rainclouds.
Sometimes they glow in moonlight
under heaped cumulus rimed with silver,
and I've seen them bright as sun-dogs
when dawn opalesced into a Sailor's Warning
across a fish-scale sky.

I open my eyes and Venus
is her masthead light.
You sleep as if curled on the nets
your head against the thwart:
your dream
dreams me on the helm.
I can circumnavigate the globe.

Signal Flag K: I wish to communicate with you

KILO

Evenings, we sit on the rocks above the bay
and watch the tides. If there are signs
of a good sunset, take a jacket and an apple.
A nod might say *the buzzard's back
on the fence post*, a small gesture
question a dark streak in the waves.
Neither of us has anything to say
significant enough to break the silence.
I think I like low springs best,
the whole bay an emptied bowl,
the uncaught moment of the turn.

In the winter we shall drag the armchairs
nearer the stove, light all the lamps
and read each other
poems we do not understand
in case sound speaks for itself.
We can take turns to fetch tea and oranges.
No one comes out here till spring.

When I live alone again and am used to fears
at night when sheep rub up against the walls
I might remember scraps of old tunes;
I might remember singing in the bath.
Wrapped in white towels I shall stare out
through my reflection at the dark sea
for red lights half a mile off, find
a faint deck-light with binoculars
and watch the night-work of tiny figures.

Signal Flag P: vessel about to put to sea

PAPA

Round the world on an almanac's
five-language glossary
stuffed at the back of a locker
in the cockpit / *kuip* / *bañera*

Checklist of all your parts
from masthead to bilge
from stem to stern /
poupe / *heck* / *popa*
your forestay and shrouds /
wanten / *obenques*
main sheet and *fokkemast*
so you know your *pujamen*
from your *gratil*

And the lifeboat of course
rettungsboot

All life's necessities
lavatory paper frying pan tinopener
nut bolt split-pin and *arandela*

Everything you'll need ashore
harbour master hospital ironmonger
for calamine lotion and
Antiseekrankheitsmittel

All you need to know about the sea
lighthouse and sunken rock
neap tide / *morte eau* and overfalls
roaring everywhere *stroomrafeling* /
stromkabbelung

Languages of danger –
gale warning backing
onshore wind squall and heavy swell
                            – and exactness
haze extensive slowly moving
at first becoming cloudy

What's missing is the word for home
absence distance loss and separation
remembrance even love

UNIFORM

I send one-line messages
that an acquaintance has died,
that your dentist has mailed a reminder.
Everything is omitted.
Can you read signal flags still?
What do I want to tell you anyway?

Days are lengthening.
The first curlew: I knew when to listen.
The geese are laying; I know where
to look for primroses under the hedge
but there's no rejoicing.
SEND. None of this was on screen.

Prayer takes many forms:
there's straw on the road for fifty yards
and disinfectant by Mealbank Farm,
more at Tom Hilton's. We go nowhere,
worry about deer, watch for signs.
Everyone dreams about disease.

Snow is forecast. The mountain shines.
All of us here are holding our breath.
We wake knowing what everyone else
is thinking. You have forgotten
circumnavigation ends
where it began.

GOLF

Diesel, and the smell of a fishing fleet.
Alleys, short cuts to the harbour.
Greylags grazing beside the road.
Wind against tide, spume blowing back
in Eynhallow Sound.

A circle of slate-brown heather in the dead grass,
sun: a moment for stones.
Blown sand drowning the hearth,
blue velvet curtains flying,
wind unveiling the plaque.

Viking graffiti. Victorian graffiti.
The rune for *far away*.
The Italians paint their homesickness
in pinks and green to ward off waters and mist.
Spray across the causeway, wrack flung through the air.

Old stories of longing for home.
No word for this longing to be at sea,
watching from the shattered cliffs.
Foul weather, no boat in sight.
Wind chill too strong to keep on keeping watch.

Signal Flag S: my engines are going astern

SIERRA

It's less than ten minutes from dockside to airfield.
Oilskins are packed, sheets coiled. Shipshape.

Herring gulls pick over nets piled on the quay for repair.
The new lifeboat dwarfs what's left of the fleet:
Sir Max Aitken's dark hull mirrors the waves: a quiet day and
they're cleaning her orange superstructure and heavy gear.

How many times have we sailed here before?
I even remembered the Beasts of Holm, though it's calm today.

I could still steer on the wind and winch the genoa
while you hoisted the main. These things come naturally.
I wonder what you are thinking, but do not ask.
Have we been trying to sail back to who we used to be?

Airborne north of Loch Marivaig under the cloud,
the white sand of Uig still in the soles of my shoes,

there's a moment that belongs to the past: a figure
waves from the deck of a small boat heading into the wind,
south, where the sea is sheet metal and the Shiants float
like two grey creatures turning their hump backs on one another.

Signal Flag J: I am on fire and have dangerous cargo: keep clear

JULIETT

Static, and background voices.
Al-lo. Al-lo. A foreign operator,
probably a wrong number
but I wanted it to be you.
Strange, to think of your life
the other side of the world.
Don't even speculate: your death
would have been simpler.

Here the barometer's holding 1047:
blue days alternate with fog.
Smokepurple buds swell on the alders;
the ganders are fighting for geese
but it's still too early for eggs.
This is what counts. This is what's real.
Is this what I would have said?
Would you have known what I meant? Over.

You sail a dream script I don't believe in,
sometimes send messages
in a language I can't speak.
We want stories to have endings:
I'll write shipwreck; I'll write typhoon.
A tidal wave will smash across the ocean,
stranding me on solid ground. Out.

OSCAR

He comes familiar, driving here
in a pair of old slippers, unmanly,
as if we are comfortable old friends.
Which we are not: the Atlantic's
between us, and many tides. He leans
towards my cheek and I lean back.

He has come about the wedding,
sits in the armchair by the stove
as if he belongs and I perform
listening body language
to words strangers could speak.

He's noticed the new table. I notice
how his hair's too short at the back,
how a red checked shirt doesn't suit,
how his eyes refuse mine.
What can I say about that?

How this will not do.
How I've been handed the wrong script:
he should go out and come in
by the other door so I can fling
my arms round the familiar
smell of him hold on until he is here.

I lean forward, offer another whisky.
The stars are showing when he leaves
and he looks up at the northern sky.
There were moments I might have made
a difference. This is not one of them.

DELTA

He rang: *Right away.*
Then: he'd fetch it in an hour;
he'd fetch it later this afternoon.
In the end I hung it on the fence,
the fleece he left here last night.
What was there to say?

I heard the car.
I was down the field,
too far to run back
and undo what I had done –
the blue shape of him
strung up like a shot crow.

Signal Flag A: I have a diver down; keep well clear at slow speed

ALPHA

It's not how I remember:
a petrol pump, a supermarket.
Alasdair is dead and Flora Ann
has been to London. Some of the townships
have voted for streetlamps – never mind stars
or the Northern Lights.

Even the weather is civilised: the sea
is blue and the wrack below the high tide line
so bright you'd think that islands rust in water.
A sleight of hand among clouds,
the sea silvers and all is grey again.
Just as it used to be.

It is I who am changed.
I sit on the grass and watch rocks and skerries
in the Sound come and go with the tides.
The long chains of islands and reefs
make sense as they never used to do
at the fairway buoy

when I strained through smirr for bearings ahead
instruments alarming as the depth fell
and I knew the *Pilot's* 'Cautions' about tidal streams,
a maze of rocks and shallow passages
and heavy seas across the northwest bar
off by heart.

I can lie in this high white bed and count
the signature of Stumbles Rock: flash 2/Red/6 seconds.

Perhaps nobody else is listening
to the engine of a small boat a mile offshore
and two seals singing out beyond Killegray.
At home it would be dark by now.

Signal Flag E/D: your distress signals are understood

ECHO DELTA

Some satellite short-circuits the Atlantic
so you can tell me you're hurt.
I remind you you've had it before:
not to rush it, roll a pillow under your neck.
You want me to know this conversation costs
however many dollars a minute.
I can hear other voices a long way off.
When you ask about things
I tell you the cloud's come down
so the air's damp and cold and
nowhere beyond the hedge exists,
and wonder if you notice
I never speak about myself.
In the silence before you reply
my tinned voice is repeating 'exists'.
When you say goodbye
the static is chorusing words
spoken before goodbye.
Don't ring off: if we keep listening
we might hear what we said
and it might sound different now.

TANGO

We exchange an unexpected tropical storm,
the sea smoking with black rain squalls
for an Indian summer,
tomatoes ripening late into October.
For his repairs to the main alternator
and forward bilge pump, I offer
a blocked sceptic tank outfall:
each of us construes a life
of small difficulties and fortitude.

We no longer speak about the past.
But nothing dissipates, energy's constant:
the storm that had him run for shelter,
put two anchors down and drop the bimini
tracked north. It veered southeast, collapsed
then re-formed in mid-Atlantic as Low G.
In two weeks' time it will rattle my doors
and break the tops off young ash trees
still heavy with this season's growth.

Signal Flag I: I am altering course to port

INDIA

A quiet click of the latch and the door
opens a little. I look up
as if you will breeze into the kitchen.
You must have been on my mind:
I heard you were back in the country.
But it's only the wind.

The first half dozen yellow leaves
skitter past the window from the birch
which lifts and sways after a week
of hold-your-breath stillness.
It's the equinox. Expect gales.
Hurricane season, over there.

No swallows. I always imagine
I'll see them leave, lined up, predestined,
all at once, but never do.
They were here only last week
– a high pandemonium
where there's now empty air.

For them there's always next year.
For you   I'm not sure

Night Snow

A light snow and it's explicit,
the history of the night.
Deer have betrayed their galleries and racks,
and crowded round high gates:
their slots depart, return, depart,
case the garden fence along the track.
The Y-pattern prints of a hare at speed
lengthen below a run through the hedge.
Four-toed runes of a heron's slow walk
track the heavy footed explorations of the geese.
Unreadable scuffs beneath the oak
and everything coming and going
along the path in Great Robin's Close,
grass showing through, and small things
going off-piste, familiar waymarks whited out.
Home, you used to say, but you
were always too hasty for any of this.

Verdict

I have decided not to forgive you.
I considered the case for several years
before judgment took me like a sneeze at haytime.

Whether you will forgive me is another matter
because I never told you what I did.
Sometimes, you said, you thought I was a witch

the way I'd turn up at bad moments,
ask innocent questions with guilty answers
and spray alarming malapropisms around.

I'd wait until you were daydreaming
or your telephone voice became urgent and staccato
or your plans were so complex they'd confuse me,

and when you were looking the other way
I'd lift the trapdoor at the back of your head
and peer inside. Simple really.

I didn't always like what I saw: too many mirrors
and tulle drapes; even on the good side,
decor a shade ostentatious.

I had a quick look when you passed by the other day:
quite a lot's been rearranged or disconnected,
some bricked up. A neat job, that.

Somewhere

there's a tent with a generous roof
and taut ropes in a field of buttercups
just like this, and you can see the fells
are turning green at last. All evening
a far drone hangs in the valley:
they're mowing the hay there too.
Someone has pasted the same row of small clouds
above the horizon, to set off
how blue, how perfect the sky, the day.

The cast is different:
they don't drive fast cars
and are not adept at guessing
the labels on each others' clothes.
Her father is faithful and listens
and she is marrying not
this one, not the one with red hair,
but the one I've imagined
who makes her laugh.

I'm there too, wearing the same green dress
and these shoes, but watch me:
I float. I sing.

Portrait

I'd no intention of taking his picture,
just a general view of the garden,
everyone talking in groups the way they do
at openings, backs to the walls, glass in hand
except this wasn't a show but they could have
looked at the flower beds and veg
in their lounge suits, pashminas and hats,
high heels and fashionable mauve.

Yet here he is in shirt sleeves,
coming round the corner of the house.
Fast. The only one not holding a glass,
trousers slipped a little and folded over his shoes.
Mouth tight: he's thinking about something,
worrying: you can see it's urgent
from the way he's leaning forward
as if to breast the winner's tape.
It's him all right. He'd hate this picture.

After the Wedding

Armfuls of wilted flowers to the compost heap,
cream stocks still fragrant in the evening damp.
Tears for the flowers, the waste, I said and you were glad
I did not mention what's unspeakable.

The lilies had lasted, and a few dark roses.
I took them to the graveyard –
startled one George Capstick of Witray
with a hot-blooded rose on his hundred year grass,
weeping, I told myself, because no one knows now,
or cares, whether he grew night-scented stocks
under the wall beside his vegetables,
or if his heart ached.

For days the smell of stocks
haunted the garden with impossibilities –
if you would change
if I could forgive you

Trace

Rough carved low down on the front
of the age-silver boskin: W + E.
Then higher, a bold WILLIAM & EDMUND.
And in flourishing cursives
where generations of milk cows
have smoothed the chamfered beam:
William & Edmund 1894.

Friends? Brothers, twins even? Lovers?
I could unearth them in the censuses among
the Williams and the Edmunds hereabouts,
trace a tithe on field names and family holdings.
Parish records for their marryings and their dying.
Perhaps they're still here side by side:
the answer engraved on a lichen-covered stone.

Always William-and-Edmund. William
could have been the stronger, inscribed himself first
while Edmund skimmed stones across the river.
Or try: William engraved his loneliness
when the older friend rode off to market or to war.
But how did he learn so elegant a script
with nested ascenders and extended serif for his W?

Swallow Scar

magpie traps
hay bob pasture topper
six foot mower
mole plough subsoiler
set of harrows
things'll look up next year

fifty sheep hurdles
electric shears treacle feeder
poultry feeders turkey plucker
eight sheets corrugated asbestos
must get round to that leak in the shed

two caravans, chassis only
four Volvo estates two Volvo cars
none with tax or MOT
come in handy for spares

threefiftythreefiftythreefifty four

four dozen breeze blocks
timber cabin without a roof,
an outside porch'll make a difference

six sixftfty sevenseven eight eightfifty

pedder boskin huddock nush
going
lambing wi' neighbour of a night
going
Robert to John, John to Robert, father to son
gone.

A Morning's Work

Ten blows. The far side
of the valley syncopates
a quiet thud back.
Three rolls of wire,
coloured these days –
if it were a car
they'd call it malachite.
Perhaps it'll fade.
Claw hammers, a bucket
of what they call *stapples*
and two chain saws.
No helmets or ear muffs
just thick red check shirts
that say everything.
The older one sights
the next post along the wire.
The younger one takes off his shirt
and picks up the whemmell.
Ten breaths, ten arcs of the back
ten shocks to the spine. Ten replies
from Harrison's side of the river.
The older one sets the next post.
I want to ask about the strainers,
about a stile into the Old Wood,
but it's all post whemmell echo
                    post whemmell echo
                            post whemmell echo

29

A Good Job

They take for granted it will be straight and true.
No one sees him board the sides
or cover spoil with sheets of astroturf.
He parks discreetly a distance off,
reading the paper, flask on the dashboard.

We agree it's a bad business.
He tells me about the digging,
easy, on shingle in the valley bottom,
wet clay on rock up here, the worst:
you'd need dynamite for under-and-over,
here they have to be side by side.
They all think they'd like the view.
They're wrong, this isn't the place,
they don't know what it's like
six foot down on your back:
Burton's best, you look up
and the spire points straight to heaven.
And the digging's clean and dry.

A good job this, outdoors, time's your own
and finished soon enough to fetch the lad
from school, watch him do his homework
so he doesn't spend his life
in cold water to his thighs like his Dad.

Another Death

You can see where they braked.
Someone must have pulled the corpse
off the road and laid it under the hedge
by the cattle grid. They always cross there.
The body is still bright, gingery.
I turn up the dark muzzle, try to stay mindful
the living would not sanction touch
on feather, hair, skin. Over the years,
I have taught myself to handle death.

I knew this deer, his routines at least,
his browse past the kitchen window
while the kettle boiled for morning tea.
I used to think he knew me: he never ran,
just stared from the long grass plumes
with sombre indifference and kept on eating.

A second deer hesitates along the margin
of the wood, maps cover and space
before a dash along the green road.
This one is taller. Four days –
I wondered how long it would be
before the territory was claimed.

Soon the air will be drenched with death.
Stiff hairs will be scattered like an old mat,
just a few rib bones to say *deer*.
Next year the only mark will be a surge
of nettles under the hedge,
and I'll be watching some other deer.

Accounts

Every day, something.
Maybe only a leaf lying on the tarmac
like a clear yellow candle flame.
Maybe just a cloud formation.
Sometimes theatre: the river
undercutting an alder on the bank
which falls: a bridge, a dare.
Or two deer kids seeming
in their crazy confusion
to have forgotten how to jump.

To have written them all down:
a page for each with a couple of lines,
a drawing, or just a map.
Half a lifetime here, that's
one hundred and fifty-six A5 notebooks,
one-and-half times my bodyweight of words
and today open
at page sixteen of the next book
                          with a snipe,
a striped arrow startling me
in the shallows of the pond.

Mostly, I leave it to memory,
expect its chancy shortcuts
to replay on cue the perfect detail.
I wonder how many out-takes
I've lost, how many thousands
of leaves I've forgotten.
At least that Jack Snipe has made it
— its low, straight flight
shooting into this future reading.
And one cherry leaf falls, perennial.

After a Pear, Wine or a Priest
(early seventeenth century saying)

There must have been a high wind in the night
before this soundless morning dropped
its heavy dew on to the lawn:
broken twigs and a first fall of leaves
tangle in the grass,
and five unaccountable pears –

ripe, with long bodies,
golden, with a netting of grey-brown russet
and white lenticels round their curving haunches;
ripe, golden,

they lie on the grass quite unbruised
under the bare amelanchier tree,
unaccountable,
as if risen – like mushrooms –

                        not fallen.

A Millennium Poem

When the leaves fell from the hawthorn
by the kitchen window, it did not look bare:
simply changed colour. The berries are so thick
everyone says *It will be a hard winter.*

A family of blackbirds thrives among this plenty –
snatching down gobful after gobful
until you'd think they'd fall out of the air
with the excess weight.
I want to open the window and shout
Hey, it's only November; there'll be hard winter yet.

Now at the month end, wind in the north
and a real frost, all the easy fruit is gone:
a thin haze of red remains on branch ends.
A bird shifts sideways along a twig,
wavers for a single haw, and flutters back.
I will not feed you my food.

In my childhood garden we had one blackbird
with a white head. Even then
everyone said *White bread –*
it's been eating too much white bread.

Amphibium

This morning he was a shadow at the bottom of the hill;
by afternoon stalking up near the picnic bench.
Now he is here looking in at me looking out.
Last night I dreamt of frogs.

He cloaks himself with grey wings
against the northerly and settles down.
I can see him as a critic, imagine opera glasses.
Watching. For me, perhaps for frogs.

We make such visitations into signs.
An upstart kestrel hovers exactly above the watcher
who shakes himself at the interruption, heaves into the air.
Zadkiel says *to dream of frogs is favourable.*

Next day he's here again. Something about
the way he circles, closes in, discomfits me
yet *he or she who dreams of frogs has friends
and a propitious season on the farm.*

Forecast

Since I stopped wearing a watch
I've not been more than ten minutes out
when someone asks the time.
I'm not sure whether it's Thursday
or Friday, but this doesn't matter
because I know exactly where the moon
three days from full will rise tonight
on the shoulder of the mountain.
It's five days since I heard the news,
but only names and places change.
These days I don't buy newpapers:
last year's are stacked behind the barn.

But I still listen to the forecast
before deciding whether to read,
to mow or plant out leeks.
It's time I was content simply
to hold up a wetted finger,
look upwind and smell the air
so I can open the back door to the morning
and fall in step with a world
that treads a measure all its own.

Reincarnation

I've arranged to come back
as an old stone outbarn
like the one down at Furnessford
with an ogee datestone 1641 for dignity
and three initials W, T & E that spell belonging.
Grade II Listed at least, to ensure I'm well preserved.

That way I'll feel the seasons.
In winter the damp breaths of heifers
will seep out through my cracks.
I'll belch methane to open the shippon door
for their grass-crazy dance in spring.
Summer breezes will wash through me
like colonic irrigation while my rafters
eavesdrop on the tinnitus of swallows.
I'll stuff myself with the sweet nostalgia of hay,
bed down for sleep in autumn.

This is not a passive choice.
I'll slip a roof slab down to crush the chainsaw
if the colloquy of trees that shelter me is under threat.
I'll harbour mildews in my boskins
be quick to rot a store of GM seeds.
I'll creak and groan, slam doors on still mornings
and make developers uneasy,
block the beck with plastic sacks
so it can sweep away the bridge
just as their lorry crosses.
I'll draw lightning down a pitch fork
to melt the bucket on their JCB.

I could loosen mortar, dislodge a stone
perhaps give house room to a soul
who's arranged to do her haunting as an owl.

Three Peaks

Pen y ghent

If it were not for this long haul
after convalescence, you would have left me
far behind by now.

Go-back, go-back, go-back,
back back back. The grouse cackle
and whirr, rout us off their lek.

It's quiet in the lee, but ice-laden top-winds
stream crystals on short grass
and scorch the skin.

The way you said it:
cheeks like ripe apricots,
as if I'm from some warm, far hill.

Ingleborough

They've stepped the mountain against wear now,
carted back the broken gate stoops, lintels
and dressed door jambs they quarried out for years.
A couple of pieces of fancy corbelling
for where the track turns.

Limewash and red paint and a letter G
— we tramp them back,
                              stone to stone,
heads down
like future archaeologists
identifying grandiose mansions
among the lithic scatters
that define a mountain top.

Whernside

I took this because of the slow curve
of the valley and the way the great viaduct
shrinks to a toy as you climb.
That's a rainbow-painted helicopter
dumping red sandhills on the snow,
as if a giant mole's tunnelled up the ridge.

But when I look back on that day,
I picture two tiny figures laughing
and brushing off the fiery ice and sparkle
his rotors baptise them with,
dark specks in the past tense
as the pilot lifts and banks away.

Thirty-six, Glossy, Four-by-six

1

Edge-to-edge berries against a glitter of sharp leaves.
That the tree I planted a quarter of a century ago
could stand dark outside the study window
and not fruit till now – had to be recorded.
As if it had suddenly decided to change sex.

2-11

A pile of stone, a kango hammer, a hole
where the hearth used to be;
rubble in the middle of the main room.
Rebuilding: a hiatus far messier
than careful accounts in a journal.

12-24

Take a picture of Edna and Mabel together.
Everyone knew what the word *together* contained
except perhaps Edna and Mabel,
smiles as hesitant as their steps
who may have chosen not to know,
leaning on each other and their sticks
so you can't tell who's supporting whom.

25-29, 30-34

The river in flood – brown and grey mud
swirled waist-high round trees on the bank.
And ice, the river stilled, frozen between rocks,
interlocked spars suspended gleaming
white in the sun and brilliantly
blue in Agfa shade.

35-36

The bonfire of last year's rubbish:
its red and charred heart, and sparks.

Thread

Somewhere in this house
a glass of red wine is collecting spiders.
I set it down only for a moment
to take a book from the shelf.
After half an hour of searching
I poured another,
but I worry about other things
I haven't remembered I've forgotten.

Last week I put cheese in the bread bin and
found unwashed socks in the freezer.
Usually, it's me I misplace –
discover I'm in the bedroom and wonder
what it is I should be doing there.
The old trick still works, but I worry
what will happen if I retrace my steps
one day to find I've lost the thread.

The Foot Thing

On your first visit, you put your feet up
on my polished table. Ankles crossed.
Doc Martens. (And this was years after
they were out of fashion with the young.)

It can't have been easy
for a small woman like you
to have kept your feet up like that.
I had to talk to you by leaning round.

I didn't know what to do –
whether to push them off, offer a cushion,
tell you I couldn't see you for your feet,
or ask if you had trouble with circulation.

I did the sort of thing I always do:
I just set a knife on one side
and a fork on the other as if that were
a customary greeting for soles

and kept my face blank.
It must have been a test, because
I never saw you do it again, not here,
not at home, not in a waiting room.

You came again so many times
I must have passed, though
feel I failed: I still don't know
what you wanted me to do.

Cyclamen

There is a window. And because it's bare
you can see through the tree
that was planted too close.
You can see a road, you say, with cars
going home. Too far away for sound.
A road and a rise behind, fields and walls.
Sometimes stray clouds against the winter sky
turn pink and you think the west must be
as deep as raspberries. Once
two figures walked along the skyline.
Free, is what you said.

You wave to a small cyclamen, white flowers
wearying over dark-hearted leaves, tell me
take it away and keep it cool:
in places like this they don't last.

Letters

It never occurred to me
to take your photograph.
I keep finding your letters inside books.

Soon I shall have them by heart
your brisk stroll up Whinskill Stones,
the walk up Crummockdale
along to Norber and back to Austwick,
the dark too soon in the afternoon.
How you burrowed into the garden again
after the too much that was London,
pruned the apples, teetered on a long ladder,
glad, you said, you only had to do it
once a year. Only a few months back.

You shaped the apples well:
branches open to the sky, bracelets of spurs.
I keep thinking I'll walk by,
find out how they're fruiting.
Someone else's harvest.

Our Lady of the Woods

The villagers expected oak.
        So she planted oak.
The gamekeeper told her
deer didn't eat ash
        so she planted ash.
The forester had a few limes
and some gean to spare
        so she planted three small-leaved limes
        and his wild cherries everywhere.
The cabinet maker had grown
some Scots pine from seed
he'd gathered up north
but had no land
where he could pay his debt.
        So she planted his pines
        on the in-by land
        like all the old farmsteads.
For superstition and small birds
        she planted rowan;
for white blossom at Easter,
        blackthorn; and whitethorn
for Whitsun;
        elder,
for the devil.

For herself
        she planted birch.
One of the old gardeners had written
If in doubt, plant a silver birch.
This pleased her.
Every time she doubted a lover
        she planted a birch.
When she was old and doubted
she'd see another spring
        she planted birch.

45

Graveyard

beloved wet grasses
dearly beloved rosebay willow herb
treasured memories of dandelion and dock
of your charity pray for the repose of the souls of
the first winded brown sycamore leaves

also
a young birch
aged 2 years and 2 months
also
a holly seedling
aged 11 weeks
also
a bird-sown rowan
who died aged 11 months

tree roots canting stones
in affectionate remembrance of lady fern
wife of brambles
and a handful of dry and seedy blackberries
relict of the above

here lieth the body
sacred

The Silvery Sea
                    sank 14th June 1998

Not in Rockall, Bailey or South East Iceland
nor in rips and overfalls off Duncansby Head;
not in storm force 10 or poor visibility;
not with light icing on the gear,
the barometer falling rapidly;
not from an open boat with canvas and oars,
in history

but now,
in the present tense
from a well-found purser more than 200 tons
with radar and GPS on a fine June morning
and in sight of the coast of Denmark,

there are empty life-rafts and an oil slick
on the silvery sea.

And the sand eels
caught for top heavy tanks
that balance the books but not nature
are back in the sands 100 feet down
taking with them Zander and Tucker,
Michael, Billy and Druimdhu,
down
to the never-named fear
they held in their hearts
(a snagged net, an ankle gripped
by uncoiling wire ropes)
– the fear that has men
never learn to swim, has them
make peace with their women
– and with their God – each time

before the isophase light
on the east end of the pier
slips past to port.

Arnol, 1875

Room for four adults and two cows,
and peat stain the only colour
in the blackhouse winter.

No window, no chimney,
just smoke clinging under the thatch.

Then it's April:
galaxies of flowers across the grazings.
You can hear crakes in the rhubarb all night.

Re-settlement

They were dying anyway
of diseases gifted by brief summer tourists
from the steamer anchored in Village Bay.
Or blame inbreeding and anointment
with fulmar oil. Or bigotry and missionaries.

For their own good said Barclay
to have their curious feet blinded by boots.
Their own good, to labour for coins
instead of necessity, to exchange belonging
for water closets and doors that locked.

I know one man survived, set to work
in that black forest called Fiunary.
Imagine *This is a tree; these, roots.*
Perhaps he strode the great cliffs of Morvern,
gazed past Mull towards the Western Isles
and saw Hirta, *fata morgana*,
trembling in pure air above the horizon.

The Crowbar and the Faggot Were Here

First

We have been removed from lands
occupied by ourselves and our forefathers;
we have been reduced to great poverty
huddled together in this miserable village.

We cannot get any land to cultivate
although abundance of good land,
overgrown with heather and rushes,
is going to waste at our very doors.

We would be glad of one cow's grass
at a reasonable rent which we could pay.
We know that the want of good milk
has a deteriorating effect upon our children.

A medical gentleman recommended
cheap beer for rearing our offspring,
but the use of such a substitute for milk
we repudiate with scorn.

Next

Under former proprietors
we had the privilege of cutting peats
as near hand as we could find them,
but now we are prevented from doing this.

The poorest and most destitute of us
dare not gather a few tufts of heather
to keep up the fire, in case the game
be put to the least inconvenience.

We are at all seasons of the year
under the necessity of buying coal
and in this remote district so far situated
from the centres of the south, coal is a luxury.

Third

The collection at our church door
of £11 sterling per annum was sufficient
to support all the poor or destitute people
within the district fifty years ago.

Today our poor rates amount to over £600
yet our population has been halved.
Such are the benefits conferred by 'economics'.
We can scarcely call our souls our own.

Last

Our Lord and Saviour said,
'How much more valuable is a man than a sheep?'
But our landlords say, 'How much more valuable is,
not even a sheep, but a game bird than a man?'

Source: Philip Gaskell, *Morvern Transformed*

Old Ardtornish I

Only one room and it's nearly all table.
When everything's done,
it's polished. That's where you sit.

Always a wind. Tonight rattling
the iron windows at the back, north,
the worst, it flickers the paraffin lamps.

Scoured pans hang under the shelf,
glow like a family of quiet moons.
The dresser's never been moved.

I've edged it far enough from the wall
to brush out the thick grey dirt.
All that I'll find of other lives.

I look and look into its mirror:
lamplight, but only now. It reflects
the stove doors, reshaped into clams.

Below the cliff, the Sound ebbs and floods,
busy with some purpose of its own
rearranging rocks at the edge of the bay.

Old Ardtornish II

Mornings, carry down the lamps,
fill them and trim the wicks.
Evenings when there's a breeze
walk down to the point
and watch for lights across the Sound.
Small rituals. Bookends.

I wonder now what I did all day.
Bring back firewood perhaps,
check the water pipe for leaks?
It took hours to fetch supplies,
climbing past the fank
and down the drovers' road.

I was careful, so far
from anywhere, and young.
The safe path to the waterfall; the boat
only on a rising tide around the bay.
Once I even walked eight miles
to telephone and say: all right.

Now I'd take the cliff path.
I'd search until I found Loch Tearnait
and swim off the rocks.
At night I'd net the fish trap
across the bay, stay out
and watch the stars.

Old Ardtornish III

I photographed the old dresser
full of life: two canisters of tea and a jug
filled with Devil's Bit and Wavy Hair Grass,
wine glasses and a bottle of Tormore
all cleverly arranged so the camera's
looking in and the mirror's looking out
on the window and the Sound shining
below the cliff. The dresser's bare now.

Upstairs the bed has gone. The heavy drawers
remain and the red-painted mirror
must have been too shabby to take.
I used to lie in bed and watch the roof light
mix leaf shadows and morning sun
across the slopes and angles of the ceiling.

The bathroom was dilapidated even then.
Now the silvering on the tiny mirror
above the basin's so blebbed and pitted
I could be a shadow passing over lichen.

One of the Places

No roof timbers. Gables still more or less square.
Most of it history, most of it guesswork, the sort of place
where everything has happened if one could decipher the wind.

Fishing perhaps, as well as the land, but only on good days.
They could have read the tides from here, two small windows
giving the time of day by floods and ebbs.

One always imagines the old would be the last to leave
but there would have been children, there would have been deaths.
Today lambs are dying here and there across the grazings.

Where could they have been buried among all this rock?
No graves, no marks: wind has scoured every stone
for leftovers and the mortar leached out long ago.

The Return

Gently, you remind me how dark are the winters.
I can see for myself the houses across the loch are silent.
I trail behind. Your boots press peat brown pools
into the moss: it must have been wet all summer long.

You are telling me how your grandfather's generation
claimed this land after the war and raised a roof
to signal ownership with chimney smoke,
and I am watching the cotton-grass blow.

We jump the lazybeds neither of us remembers worked,
and crush the sweet medicinal smell from bog myrtle
your mother always leaved between clean linen,
green among white, green among white,

white on the green, white on the green,
sheep's wool rainwashed clean, and bones bleached
where the raven dropped them on cropped turf.
No more histories or regrets, I want to tell you

stop, here, on this bedrock: let the wind blow through us.
Let's watch guillemots dive, guess where they'll surface.

A Tide Watch. The Rule of Twelfths.

Low tide
Cloud come down. Seascape of greys
as fine rain washes colour away.
Oarweed out west of the bay sways and glistens.
Small breezes fall from the low cliff to scuff the sea.
Slack water. *Tidal constant:*
Dover minus 5 hours 15.

First twelfth
Flood sets north.
Every few seconds an impulse
from a small pool in the centre of the bay
runs up the slip, a last Atlantic memory.
The unsharp horizon hints at islands.

Quarter
Water spreadeagles into the bay,
and frisks rock fallen round the sides.
Drizzle and chimney-smoke tumble
together to the water's edge,
streak across the bay and out to sea.
Winds may raise sea level, advance high water.

Half-tide
The flick of a tail: otter,
fishing where tide rips at the entrance .
Fingers of rock belie geology,
seem to float and mimic seals.
Channel-wrack paints an orange waterline
along the cliff. *Mean range springs 4·3 metres.*
Drizzle flattens the sea.

Three quarters
The bay fills to its horseshoe shape,
small waves careening on the pebble beach.
Neaps would stop at this.
Tidal cycles are regular
but these precise calculations of ebb and flow
are of no account to the sea.

Last twelfth
Rain heavy, the horizon a shift in the light.
Foam licks at lichens on the splash line.
Tide times and heights vary from predictions:
always err on the cautious side.

High springs
The bay replete, a deceptive pool
at the edge of a breaking Sound.
The weather will change with the tide
and it does, worsens, closes in
so there's nowhere else but the bay.
Drop anchor. *Pay out chain*
to five times tidal rise.
Stop the moon.

The Rule of Twelfths: one twelfth of a tide
moves in each of its first and last hours; two
twelfths in its second and fifth hours and three
twelfths in each of the third and fourth hours.